peer program for youth

ARDYTH HEBEISEN

A GROUP INTERACTION PLAN TO DEVELOP

SELF-ESTEEM
SELF-UNDERSTANDING
AND COMMUNICATION SKILLS

FOREWORD BY MERTON P. STROMMEN

AUGSBURG PUBLISHING HOUSE
MINNEAPOLIS, MINNESOTA

PEER PROGRAM FOR YOUTH

Contents

FOREWORD by Merton P. Strommen 5

INTRODUCTION 7

GUIDELINES FOR LEADERS 11

WEEKEND RETREAT 19

    Segment One 20

    Segment Two 24

    Segment Three 33

    Segment Four 35

SESSION 1: Exploring Meaningful Relationships—I 39

SESSION 2: Exploring Meaningful Relationships—II 47

SESSION 3: Identifying My Strengths 53

SESSION 4: Using My Strengths 59

SESSION 5: Learning to Listen 65

SESSION 6: Communicating Your Own Feeling 75

SESSION 7: Polishing Up Communication Skills 85

SESSION 8: My Response to Others 95

SESSION 9: Values and Acceptance for Others and for Me 101

SESSION 10: Where I Go from Here 107

ACKNOWLEDGEMENTS

A number of forces converged to bring this book into being.

There was the active search of Youth Research Center to develop and find funding for a project designed to reach out to alienated youth.

Then there was the positive response of the National Institute of Mental Health to the Youth Research Center proposal, and the subsequent funding that made Project YOUTH possible.

The proposal regarding Project YOUTH designated that one of the interventions to be designed and included would be built on the work and basic concepts of the Achievement Motivation Program as it was developed through the W. Clement and Jessie V. Stone Foundation. The stress of the Achievement Motivation Program on positive reinforcement was acknowledged as a significant and promising direction to pursue in work with youth.

An additional component which was needed for such a program was the building of communication skills. The work of Dr. Thomas Gordon in Parent Effectiveness Training was adopted as a model.

As I retrospectively view the series of events leading to the building of the PEER program, one person stands out as a central figure. Dr. Roland Larson, of Youth Research Center, was personally responsible for introducing me to and involving me in Achievement Motivation Program and Parent Effectiveness Training. It was he who suggested that I be involved in the design of the PEER program, and he offered consultation and support throughout the design and development phase of the training program.

Other persons deserving special mention include the eleven young adults who shared the task of making PEER work; the many high school youth who participated in the experimental phase of PEER; Dr. Alan Anderson, who made recommendations regarding closure of the series and generalization of learnings to relationships outside the group; Dorothy Williams, who worked skillfully with revisions and preparation for publication; and Merle, Nena, and Dieter Hebeisen, my family, each of whom experienced the whole process out of their own unique relationship with me.

ARDYTH HEBEISEN

Foreword

This book is about helping a group of young people grow toward realizing their potential as persons while forming a cohesive support group. If conscientiously and completely carried out, the program presented here will result in young people feeling better about themselves and others. More than that, it will provide them with skills for relating successfully to others, not least young people who seem headed for a life of unhappiness, delinquency, or personal tragedy.

The author, Ardyth Hebeisen, who has been related to our Youth Research Center over a period of years, has the capacity to ignite a group through her leadership. Some of her infectious and warm spirit is manifest in the program she has put together.

The program's accent is defined by its name, PEER—*P*ositive *E*ducational *E*xperiences in *R*elationships. It contrasts with encounter or sensitivity group approaches by being a structured series of educational experiences that focus on the *strengths* and *potentials* of young people.

Developed as part of a three-year research study carried out by Youth Research Center, PEER is one of the three training programs used in Youth-Reaching-Youth, a project funded by the National Institute of Mental Health, #17615. The purpose of this field experiment was to test the relative effectiveness of three educational programs: a one-to-one approach, a group skills approach, and PEER. The goals common to these programs are to develop interpersonal skills, self-esteem, openness, and interpersonal trust.

The three-year study (1970-73) shows that a major characteristic of young people who volunteer for a program of reaching out is a value orientation that motivates them into a helping role. But they are not supermen. They are not equipped with the skills to focus or carry out that concern effectively; they are harried and blessed by all the usual adolescent problems with life; they are typical in the range of their religious values, concerns, and involvements.

What measurable benefits can be expected for young people who take part in this program? Those who participated in **PEER** showed a striking increase in self-esteem, along with an increase in openness to people and to new ideas. After their participation they worried less about their own personal faults, about being loved, and about academic problems than they did when the study began. In other words, they showed a measurable gain in self-confidence. Another particular strength of PEER training is the way it develops a strong support group and motivates young people to participate actively in the group of which they are a part.

The program as presented here begins with a weekend retreat and is continued through ten evening sessions. We consider the program adaptable for use in the organizational structures of school, church, or community agency. Although a group leader with some training and skill in group leadership probably could use this book to lead a group through each of the program steps, I believe the program will have greater effectiveness if a leader first experiences the program in a training session under the leadership of a PEER trainer. Youth Research Center, 122 West Franklin, Minneapolis, makes these sessions available.

My belief is that this program, well carried out, can have a profound and lasting effect for good on the persons being trained, and their group. Beyond these gains, however, I see hope for youth reaching youth in more meaningful ways, in a society where thousands of lonely youth are waiting for a friend who is committed to being a friend.

When used in a congregational setting, the value of this program can be enhanced if the leader relates some of the meaningful group experiences to theological concepts of the church. The big words of theology—love, forgiveness, fellowship, Holy Spirit, sin— take on new meaning when related to provocative experiences. Learning theology in this way helps participants see that beliefs, like theory, can be extremely practical and life-related. Christian beliefs deal with the issues of life.

MERTON P. STROMMEN

President, Youth Research Center

Principal Investigator of Project Youth

INTRODUCTION

PEER is a group interaction program for groups of from six to twelve members. It is designed to enable its participants to

- build a better self-understanding or self-image
- build a better understanding of others
- encourage greater acceptance of and pleasure in what we and others are ("I'm OK—You're OK")
- teach communication skills which maximize awareness of
  what I am experiencing
  what I perceive you to be experiencing

In its design PEER makes prominent use of positive reinforcement as modeled in the Achievement Motivation Program and communication concepts patterned after work done by Dr. Thomas Gordon in Parent Effectiveness Training.

The title of Thomas Harris's book, *I'm OK—You're OK,* communicates the basic assumption of PEER. At the core of who we are, we are each acceptable as persons. From a belief that "I'm OK—You're OK" we can turn to each person we interact with and openly deal with their attitudes, values, feelings, and behaviors. We can affirm the OK-ness of their having their own perceptions, their own feelings, and we, ours. Within this basic sense of acceptance, the divergence of another person from your set of norms can be responded to with less defensiveness and rejection.

Positive reinforcement is another central concept in PEER. "I'm OK—You're OK" is essentially a basic interpersonal attitude which is a form of positive reinforcement. Over and over again in the program, participants will have opportunities to communicate to one another messages that affirm each person's uniqueness, capability, lovability. A primary goal is to enable each person participating to gain and to strengthen his own awareness of his strengths, constructive aspects of his life style, and who he is. We

7

commonly think of ourselves as we believe others think of us, and this is an important cue to the program. In PEER we are attempting to revise for ourselves what we think others think of us, to begin to hold a more constructive and positive view of ourselves.

Some assumed values of PEER are:

- Both the good and the bad exist in life. We recognize the bad, we deal with it, but, basically, we choose to focus on and celebrate the good, the positive, the emotions and experiences which help us transcend self-defeating negative attitudes.

- All people at core are acceptable.

- The uniqueness of each person is special, worth sensing and celebrating. It is not necessary to be like all the others to be what one "ought" to be.

- Rejection, shame, "Not OK" feelings and communications interfere with growth and a healthy, wholesome way of being a person.

- The more congruent (honest and open) a person is, the more whole, and, in the long run, the more effective he will be in personal relationships.

- Honesty is desirable. Masking real feeling or manipulation and exploitation of others are not desirable.

- Empathic skill, the ability to sense and respond to what another person is feeling, is a desirable quality.

- It is good to understand and share meanings, perceptions, and experiences between people.

- It is desirable to be able to make a decision to do something and then carry it out. Goal-directedness is valued.

Outline of the Program

The series is designed to begin with a structured weekend retreat which focuses on getting acquainted and building trust, caring, and openness among the members. The retreat is followed by ten $2\frac{1}{2}$ hour sessions which are structured with four elements in each session. Here is a description of the four elements.

GOAL SETTING

Through setting goals and meeting them, self-confidence and a sense of success are built. This also provides a framework for achieving relationship goals later in the project.

A PRIMARY TASK

This is the major task for each meeting and may focus on building self-image, improving communication skills, or clarifying personal value systems as they relate to self-perception and relationships.

BASIC CONCEPTS

Usually presented in mini-lecture style, these are designed to be a description of some of the factors involved in building relationships.

SKILL DEVELOPMENT

This is usually built into the primary task as well as other transactions among members. Focus is on listening, self-disclosure, and various applications of these skills.

BASIC ELEMENTS OF RETREAT AND WEEKLY SESSIONS

Session	Goal Setting	Main Task	Conceptual	Skill Development
Retreat	Set own goal for weekend	Play, share, learn to know one another	Basic relationship building concepts	Increasing awareness of self and others
1	Introduce goal concept; set goal for the week	Relationship Survey	Sharing Me, Sharing You, Really listening	Self-disclosure, Sensing another's feelings
2	Goal report, goal setting	Relationship Survey-summarizing	Trust in relationships	Gaining greater awareness of our relationship needs
3	Goal report, goal setting	Strength bombardment. What are my strengths?	Your perception of me can hinder or help	Hearing another's perception of me
4	Goal report, goal setting	Strength bombardment. How can I better use my strengths?	Self-perception and relationships	Sharing how I see you
5	Goal report, goal setting	Build communication skills, Listening to another's feelings	Listening for the message	Reflective Listening
6	Goal report, goal setting	Build communication skills, Sharing my feelings	Value of honestly sharing my feelings with you	Self-disclosure as valid basis of response to another
7	Goal report, goal setting	Practicing relationships with people in need	Power of acceptance	Mixing use of reflective listening and "I" messages
8	Goal report, goal setting	People with qualities I like or dislike		Continued self-disclosure
9	Goal report, goal setting	Identifying what I value in life. Can I accept you and me?	You and I may value life on a different basis	Communicating of acceptance
10	Goal report long range goals	Build a support base in other places	Thinking about application of these skills in other places	

GUIDELINES FOR LEADERS

PEER is a packaged, pre-designed program. As a leader of PEER your primary function is to provide a climate for the group experiences and to take a kind of administrative role by guiding the group through them.

Your responsibility is to:

- introduce, bring to a close, and tie together the experiences included as a part of the PEER program
- to be a task-oriented time keeper who keeps the group moving through the experiences so they don't get sidetracked
- to restate and call attention to the main ideas in the program to help focus learning
- to set a climate of acceptance, openness, warmth, providing an environment which encourages people to be free, to be genuine, and to grow
- to share in a common experience and a give-and-take in relationship with the members
- to serve as an anchor point, as one who is reliable and trustworthy and responsible for the group
- to be open with the group regarding questions or issues which affect the group. Example: if a member drops out, deal with it in the group.

Let the program do the rest.

Here are some specific cues to you as leader.

1. Some groups seem to need a stronger leadership role to guide them through the experiences. Every group is different, but you can be prepared to offer some direct strong leadership with some groups, while others need only a suggestion from the leader to move them along the outlines of the program.

2. Encourage your group members to be honest and open in all their transactions in the group within the limits of what is comfortable for them. Comfort level is an important thing to emphasize. If they push themselves too far past their own sense of comfort, the experience may be too stressful and will have a

11

negative rather than a positive effect on their increasing ability to be open in appropriate settings. Pushing them too far too fast can slow rather than encourage growth. Encourage each member to be sensitive to what he is comfortable with and what his needs are, and to manage his own actions in the group on the basis of what he feels is best for him. What you are attempting to build is a challenging setting where he is encouraged and supported for reaching out and growing, but where he is accepted for what and where he is and free to move at his own pace.

3. Your relationship with your group members is an important factor in the process of your group. Four elements can firm up your effectiveness in your group:

   • Both you and the members have something to gain from the relationship.

   • You have a capacity to understand and feel what your members are feeling.

   • Your behavior is such that your group members can consider you as reliable and sound.

   • You and your members have enough shared experiences to provide a base for common understanding. The shared experiences may be created together, as in a retreat experience or through common experiences in your lives such as similar home background, education.

4. Model the skills and personal characteristics you wish to teach — trust, openness, honesty, warmth, congruence. Be this kind of person whenever you can and still be genuinely who you are. Make the communication skills, the whole matter of acceptance of self and others, a part of your way of life and relating to other people. When you do this, you help make it safe for others to do the same.

5. Be sensitive to the feelings of your group members, but be aware of what feelings you are picking up from them and what feelings are your own. You want to be empathetic with them, but maintain your own base for feeling.

6. Enthusiasm is an important leader characteristic — and contagious! But, most important of all, be genuine in all you do.

7. Know and understand your material well. When you introduce new tasks, do it carefully and check to see that your instructions are understood by those attempting to carry them out.

8. Provide transitions from one part of the evening's sessions to another by reviewing the foundations of what has just gone before in two or three sentences as you lead into a new thing.

9. Frequently refer back to charts and key ideas to help make the overall concepts of the course tie in with the subject under discussion.

10. Time limitations may sometimes be a problem in this series. If they are, hold your group to the content and intentions of the sessions and avoid a lot of extraneous talking.

11. Make an effort to tie in all experiences to the group member's past experiences or his personal feelings. The experience is more meaningful then and learning occurs more quickly.

12. Use your sense of timing about
    • when to move on in the session
    • when to continue sharing in something that feels important to the group
    • when someone has a problem.

13. When one of the members of the group seems to be particularly reticent, you need to be sensitive to the possibility that he is having some problem related to his participation in the program. Then you need to discriminate whether you can wait until he comes to you about his concern, or whether you should approach him about it.

14. As you lead, try to enter your relationship with the group as a joint learner. When, as a group or as individuals, you come up with a problem (how to transfer relationships in the group to experiences outside the group, for example) share the search

for a solution with the group. Provide a setting in which you can talk freely about the issues, without feeling pressured to come up with a solution. Instead conduct a search. "Let's share. We may create our own answers. I'm not an expert."

15. You need to have accurate information about how your group is going. A simple way of getting this information is to ask the members of the group for their reactions to the experiences they are having in the group.

16. Each member of a group can increase his learning and his effectiveness in contributing to the growth of the group if he pools his strengths with other members of the group. When any person senses a lack in the group or a dissatisfaction with what's happening right now, he can give what he has to give as he senses it. Some contributions will be

  • being sensitive to when the group is getting side tracked and needs to move on with the task as hand
  • offering insights to the group on what they are experiencing together
  • making arrangements for activities, meeting places, etc.
  • providing softness, kindness, warmth or support to other members

An important key for each participant is to be sensitive to what is happening and to what he can offer to that situation in the group.

17. The style of closing for each weekly meeting is important to the maintenance of good feeling in the group, but because closings must fit individual groups they are hard to prescribe. At the end of Session 1 you might discuss in the group how members want to feel as they start home, and how they would like to accomplish this. At subsequent sessions it will be helpful if the leader, knowing his group, does some thinking in advance about what the mood is likely to be at the session's end, and has several alternative plans in mind for closing. Here are some possibilities:
  Sing a favorite song.
  Sing a silly song, and walk out singing.

Everybody collect in a group hug.
Hold hands in a circle for a minute of silence
Each member agree to say good night to every
   person present, using the person's name
Repeat together a favorite quote, or line of
   poetry, or legend from a favorite poster

There are many others; these are a few. The two important points are that (1) you do something that gives a feeling of completeness to the meetings, and (2) what you do fits the group personality and the members' present feelings.

18. These sessions provide time and setting and structure to encourage the growth of relationships. For some in the groups, these will be among the most meaningful relationships they have known. Because of the newness of this kind of relationship, and the strength and good feelings it provides for people in the group, some issues which arise for them may need to be discussed.

Romantic developments may be a factor in some groups. Here two people have experienced a new, powerful thing with others and have focused on one another as an important source of support, admiration, and warmth.

Affection among members of the group can be handled as a natural, easy thing. A heavy, one-sided emotional involvement can be handled kindly and with caring, and acceptance. It's OK to love or be loved intensely. Just let it be with an honest, open recognition of what it is and what it means to each person emotionally invested in the situation.

19. A major task for each individual is *transferring the relationship skills* learned in the group to relationships outside of the group. This can be discussed with the group periodically. As they share their successes and difficulties in attempting to put the same skills to work for them elsewhere, they will work out ways of identifying where and with whom they can use their skills most readily.

20. PEER should not be urged on people who don't want to participate in it. Youth who are involved in the program and

then decide that they wish to drop out should not be pressured to continue. If participants in a group start failing to attend or want to drop out: talk to them, and try to understand why they are not attending. Try to understand "where they're at" in regard to themselves and the program. If it seems that the program is somehow not fitting their needs, support them in their decision to drop out or ease off, if this is what they feel is best for them. The important key to this is, "You are acceptable. This program is for people who want it—people whose needs are met through the program. If the program doesn't fit you right now, it's not worthwhile for you to stick with it. Your needs are the most important thing." Let them make the decision based on what they think is best for them.

People may feel rejected by the group when they drop out. Continue to offer your friendship to them. It's important that they don't feel dropped as *people* because they have dropped from the program. The leader carries a special responsibility to these members so their dropping out can be experienced as constructively as possible. Ideally other members of the group could see them and do things with them when they go out with friends.

21. Enjoy yourself and your relationship with the people you are sharing PEER with.

SELF-RATING CHECK LIST

Just to keep yourself on course, here is a list of questions you might ask yourself after each segment of the weekend retreat, and after each weekly session.

Did I:

	YES	NO
Know the material?		
Keep the group to the task?		
Respond sensitively to the needs of the group?		
Feel comfortable and relaxed in what I was doing?		
Behave in a congruent (open and honest) manner?		
Convey a generally positive tone in the meeting?		

WEEKEND RETREAT

The weekend retreat is an important means for launching PEER. It creates a sense of enthusiasm and enables members of the group to begin to develop a sense of group earlier and more solidly than can be done without the weekend. The series of experiences for the retreat are presented here in the sequence in which they should occur. Approximate times needed to carry out each segment are listed. Specific time designations are not made since some groups may prefer to begin on a Friday night, others on a Saturday morning. It is important to provide plenty of time for recreation, parties, hiking, or other activities during the weekend.

Facilities Needed

Physical surroundings can be an important contribution to an experience. For the experiences designed for this weekend you should have a carpeted room which is adequately ventilated and kept at a comfortable temperature. Much of the work can be carried out sitting on the floor, so furniture is not an important feature. Groups generally have a better experience if the retreat is an overnight, away from the usual activities and environment the participants are accustomed to.

Broad Objectives for the Retreat:

- To learn how to learn from experience. PEER will be a much better experience if the participants are conscious of it as a learning experience, if they occasionally stop to ask themselves: What did I learn from that? How might I act differently because of what I know now?

- To give group members some feeling for the kinds of things we'll be doing during the PEER series.

- To share some initial experiences in self-disclosure.

RETREAT: SEGMENT ONE

Orientation

As soon as your group has arrived and settled at your retreat center, explain to them the general schedule of the weekend.

Describe some of the general purposes of the retreat:

- launch the PEER program
- give us a chance to get to know each other better
- learn to feel more comfortable with one another in a group

The weekend, and, for that matter, the whole series of experiences in the coming weeks, is designed as an educational approach to learning more about themselves and about each other, with a special focus on relationships.

Introductions with the Name Game

PURPOSE: to learn names

to have fun

to release tension

to begin getting acquainted

Start at any point in the group (preferably with a person who will follow the instructions easily—or with yourself). Participation can move clockwise or counter-clockwise around the circle. Have the first person give his first name and something that is different about him or something most people in the room probably don't know about him. The next person should repeat the first person's name and special information and then give his own name and something about himself. The third person then tells the name and special information about persons one and two and then gives his own name and something about himself—and so on until the last person in the circle names every person in the group. When you have gone completely around the group, ask if anyone would like to try it again to see if he can get all the names.

Although this works best in a group who do not know one another's names, it also works very well with groups who do, and who enjoy identifying the new piece of information with each person.

Sharing in Two's

PURPOSE: to help people be more at ease with one another if they have not been previously acquainted

to provide an experience for a beginning relationship

Have each person find a partner whom he knows less well than other members of the group. For a period of from three to five minutes, have them talk about "Some things I really enjoy doing."

Now have everyone find a new partner. This time spend five minutes talking about "People that I really like." (Describe the people.)

How I Feel About Being Here, My Expectations

PURPOSE: to make the total group more comfortable

to set a norm of sharing and self-disclosure

to begin dealing with the experience of what's happening right now

to create a readiness for being able to share

Gather the group in a circle. Point out that every person here probably has somewhat different feelings about being here and differing ideas about what might happen or what he would want to happen. Talk honestly about your own feelings at the present moment.

Moving one by one around the circle, ask each person to tell briefly how he feels about being here.

When everyone has responded, move around the circle again, with each person talking about what he expects to happen this weekend.

Purposes for the Weekend

PURPOSE: to help set expectations

to provide participants with enough information so they can begin to formulate their own commitment to the group

You might say something like this:

We've talked some about what you have expected or hoped would happen this weekend. Now I'd like to share with you a little of what we have planned, what the retreat will be like, and what we hope it will accomplish. We'd like to:

- *increase knowledge about one another and caring for one another*
- *foster group closeness*

We'll do this through a series of sharing experiences. While sharing, we'll try to be as honest and open as possible, without going beyond our comfort level. Hopefully, as time goes on we'll feel more and more comfortable about sharing together. We each can decide for ourselves what's comfortable for us, and ease off when we want to. We'll be doing a lot of talking, some drawing, and sometimes we'll do some things without talking.

Is there anything you would like to discuss about this? (Discuss any questions that come up.)

Setting Your Own Goal for the Weekend

PURPOSE: to enable each participant to have a sense of commitment to some aspect of the weekend

This is an invitation for each person to think of what he wants to experience from the weekend and to set a goal for himself. Then independent of what the program is or the group experience is, each person will also have his own goal which he has set for himself. In this way each person makes the experience his, to meet some of his needs.

Invite people to set goals which do not depend on your behavior or the behavior of specific persons in the group to complete.

Examples: I'm going to be friendly to at least five people today and tomorrow.

I'm going to listen and ask questions until I get a clear idea of what the program is about.

I'm going to enjoy myself swimming.

I'm going to get to know one person well.

Give the group a couple of minutes so each one can select for himself what he wants out of the weekend. This is a goal which they may keep to themselves if they wish. There is no group sharing with it.

RETREAT: SEGMENT TWO

If this segment is started on the morning of the second day you may begin with the *Name Game* and *Where I Am*. These two tasks are useful in getting a group back in touch with one another. *Where I Am* is a recommended task for beginning each day the group meets. If Segment Two is to follow Segment One on the same day of the retreat, begin with *What I Like About People in This Room*.

Name Game
PURPOSE: to firm up the memory of names in the group

to provide a re-entry exercise

Ask people in the group if they remember the names of everyone in the group since they played the *Name Game*. Give people who are interested a chance to see if they can recall all the names accurately.

Where I Am
PURPOSE: to strengthen the practice of self-disclosure and openness

to help members become more at ease with each other by sharing the feeling base from which they are entering the group at this moment

Explain that a group functions better when each member has some understanding of how each other person in the group is feeling. This gives a sounder base for reacting to one another when they start working together.

Example: If I have told you that I am especially happy—or depressed—today, that helps you to be more understanding and comfortable with my reactions to you when we're together.

As leader, you go first to show how it's done. In just a word or a couple of sentences share with the group how you are feeling right now. Then each person shares around the circle. When it seems appropriate or needed, offer a few words of support or reflect the feeling of members who appear to be particularly stressed.

What I Like About People in This Room

PURPOSE: to encourage the giving of positive feedback

to encourage a sense of acceptance in the group

to elicit information about non-verbal cues to provide a lead into non-verbal experiences

Point out that the PEER series will put a great deal of emphasis on the positive—the good things we experience, the things we enjoy and appreciate. Then ask the group to talk about some of the things they have noticed about each other that they like. Ask them to look around the room at the people there and describe some of the things they like. Carry on a brief group discussion highlighting these things.

Introduction to Non-Verbal Exercises

PURPOSE: to provide a rationale to members for participating in non-verbal tasks

to provide a framework from which to begin using non-verbal experiences as a means for learning

Reflect back on the conversation the group just had on things they like about one another. How many of these had to do with the way someone acts, something special they did, an impression they made or how they look? Comparatively, how many focused on what someone *said?* Comment on this. Many significant things that happen between people occur through *non-verbal* communication. The way we act is a powerful way of expressing what we feel.

Explain that the group will be spending the next segment of time exploring some of the non-talking ways people use to communicate. They will be given a series of learning experiences during which they will not talk. Instead they will be concentrating their awareness on the effects of things that happen without words.

Statue Building

PURPOSE: to create an initial awareness of how body postures communicate meaning

to do it in an enjoyable way

Tell the group that this experience is a way of exploring some ways our body postures communicate feelings.

Ask people to find partners. One partner will be the statue builder. The other partner is the building material he will use to create his statues. Ask the partners to choose which of them will be the statue builder.

Explain that you will call out a feeling or situation, and the job of the statue builder is to move his partner into a physical posture that expresses this feeling or situation. Show them how they can move their partner's arms, legs, head, to express the word you give them.
You could model this by picking out someone in the room to serve as material for you to build a statue expressing one of the words.

Then call out one of the other situations or feelings listed below and give the pairs time to build their statue.

Situations	*Feelings*
dancing	tired
waiting	happy
very sleepy	discouraged
got rich quick	ignored
	tranquility
	thinking
	joy
	grief
	amusement
	mockery
	jealousy
	giddy

When each pair has built their statue, invite people to look around at what they have built. Statues can move eyes, but not bodies.

Then switch roles for the partners. This time let the statue builder become the materials and the person who was the building material the first time become the statue builder.

Now give each pair a different feeling to build a statue for. Whisper to each pair the feeling they are to model so the others do not hear. One at a time have each pair take turns building their statue. Then have the group try to guess what the statue expresses. You could spend some time talking about the cues people are picking up that cause them to be able to identify the feeling.

If you want to have a brief group discussion about the experience, you might ask them to talk about what kinds of feelings they felt being communicated through the statues, and then check with the statues: did their own feelings begin to match the physical position they were in, after they had held that position for awhile?

Happenings Without Words

PURPOSE: to practice communicating feelings about an experience without words

to explore both talking and non-talking ways of responding to other people's feelings

Explain that during this experience we will be exploring both positive and negative kinds of feelings and looking at some ways we react to these in ourselves and in others.

This exercise will be carried out with partners. Ask group members to pick someone different from the partner they had for the statue building.

You might introduce it like this:

I am going to name some situations that may come close to something you have experienced at some time. I would like you to

27

pick one of these situations. When you have picked your situation, you will be showing your partner how you felt by acting it out. Make your own choice of situation. You and your partner need not choose the same one.

Now I'll read the situations for you to choose from. Imagine that after one of these situations has happened, you are sitting alone in your room, where it is safe to show the way you feel. Don't use any words. Just do what you think you'd do.

- *There was something you wanted very badly (a role in a play, a spot on the team, a position in the band), and you found out today you didn't get it.*

- *There was something you wanted very badly (a role in a play, a spot on the team, a position in the band), but thought you had very little chance at it—and you got it!*

- *You wanted very much to go on a weekend ski (or camping) trip with several of your friends. Your parents have told you you have to stay home, work in the yard, and babysit with your younger brother.*

- *Think of some achievement, election, or honor you'd really like. You have just won it.*

- *You have been feeling down all day—really depressed. Now two of your friends walk past and ignore you—don't even seem to notice you're there.*

- *You have been feeling down all day—really depressed. Now someone you admire, but rarely have much contact with, stops and talks, and seems to be really interested in you.*

Give the group time for each person to pick a situation. Then ask the partners to choose who will express their situation first, and who will be observer.

Then give these instructions:

To the partner acting out his situation:

Think for a minute about the situation you have chosen. Try to get into those feelings, so you are feeling them as much as you can. Then, without using any words, act the way you think you would act. Assume that you are in your room alone. So far as you know, nobody is there; you are free to let your feelings show.

To the observing partner:

Think of yourself as being the invisible man, or a mouse in the corner, observing. Be very sensitive to the other person's feelings. Try to understand and experience with him what he is feeling now. Do not talk. Only try to feel what he seems to be feeling.

All members of the group do this at the same time. When partners have had ample time to experience the shared situation, ask them to stop and quickly review in their minds what they were feeling and experiencing. For the observing partners, what did they see? What did they sense the other person feeling?

For the acting-out partners, what were they feeling? Did they think they were expressing the feelings through what their body was doing?

Now invite the total group to share what they experienced and observed. Observers who wish may comment on what their partners did, and what that communicated to them. Invite the partners who were acting out their situations to talk about their feelings. They might like to check with their observers to see if what they thought they were expressing came through.

Next:

To the observing partner:

What did you want to do in response to your partner as he was expressing his feeling? Talk about this to your partner and to the group. How would you respond to the acting-out partner with words? How could you respond to him without words?

To both partners:

Now go back into your pair and carry out the situation again. This time the observer is visible, present in the room. This time the observing partner can respond to the acting-out partner either with words or in some non-talking way. The part-

ner acting out the situation should do whatever he feels like doing in response to what his observer offers to him in words or actions.

Provide a brief time (at least 5 minutes) for the pair to re-enact the situation.

Talk about it for a few minutes in the total group. If some touching has occurred during this exercise, you might spend some time exploring:

What does touching in our group mean? Outside the group, touching may have had predominantly sexual overtones. Here is a different use of touching. What does touching mean outside our group—can we touch others outside the group with the same kind of meaning that we understand for it here?

Now have the partners switch roles. This time the observing partner will act out a situation. Check out with the group whether they want you to read the list of possibilities again.

NOTE TO THE LEADER: It may be that *Statue-Building* and *Happenings Without Words* have produced all the learnings your group is ready to absorb at this moment relative to the relationship between verbal and non-verbal communication. If that is true, you may want to omit the next two exercises. If you think they are ready for more, choose one or the other of the two following exercises. *All Together—Words and Actions* will take longer than *Looking at Us Now* and may also elicit more learning.

All Together—Words and Actions

PURPOSE: to put together two means of expression: talking about something that means a lot and acting that way, too

to explore areas of listening, talking, and acting in which participants can work to communicate more fully and freely

Explain to the group that when we are communicating with people about things that matter a lot to us, we use our words, our voices, our eyes, and all of our body actions to say what we mean.

Invite the group to select new partners. Suggest that this is a partner with whom you will be sharing something that is special to you and will be private between the two of you. Give the following instructions:

> *The last experience we had was an effort to help each of us put our actions to work in sharing information and feelings with another person. Now we'll see what happens when we use both words and actions. Choose something to tell your partner about that you have some pretty strong feelings about—something you are worried about, some decision that's hard to make, something you really get steamed up about—some unfairness or injustice against you, something neither of you need talk with anyone else in the group about. As you are talking and listening to each other, try to be somewhat aware of the actions that go with the words. What do your eyes do? How are you sitting that shows how you feel? What do your hands do? Pay some attention to these things, but don't let them get in the way of what you are saying.*

Give the partners a minimum of 15 minutes to talk. Halfway through this time period, suggest that the partners switch the talking and listening roles.

Now ask them to share with each other what the experience was like: What happened with their eyes? Did their body positions change during the conversation? What connection did these have with the way they were feeling at the time, or with what they were talking about?

Now draw the group into a circle and invite them to talk about the part of this experience that they wish to share. What did they learn about the non-word part of communication?

31

Looking At Us Now

PURPOSE: to observe nonverbal cues among the group during a final discussion

After the discussion period following the sharing in pairs is finished, lead the group into considering and observing their own physical postures at the present moment. Suggest to them that they look around the room to check what they see, and then ask them to comment on what they think is being communicated by the way members of the group are sitting at the present moment.

RETREAT: SEGMENT THREE

If this segment is started on the morning of the second day, you may begin with the *Name Review* and *Where I Am* as described at the beginning of Segment Two. Follow the instructions provided in Segment Two and then continue with *Who Am I?* If Segment Three is to follow Segment Two on the same day of the retreat, begin with *Who Am I?*

Who Am I?

PURPOSE: to provide opportunity to begin practicing disclosure, sharing of self, and sharing of what is special to others.

This is an opportunity to attempt to describe on paper who we are and share it with others in the group. Invite each member of the group to take a large sheet of newsprint and fold it in half. On the outside they are to draw something that will demonstrate in some way how they think they look on the outside—how others see them. On the inside, they are to draw something which tells what they think they are really like on the inside. Take a piece of newsprint and demonstrate this to them so they are clear about the instructions. Answer any questions they have.

Provide plenty of crayons and newsprint and give them 20 to 30 minutes until their drawings are done.

Assemble the group to share the results of the drawing. To start, select one of the members who talks readily. Follow him with other members as they volunteer, or pick them at random.

After each person has shown and described his drawing, the group may discuss their feelings and response to the drawing and the information shared through it.

Examples: "Now that you've told me that, I feel . . ."
"Here are some things I noticed in your drawing that also tell me something about you."

33

The explanation and discussion of each picture may take up to 20 minutes each.

Some groups post their pictures on the wall as each one is completed.

Gifts to Who You Are

PURPOSE: to enable other members in the group to respond to each person on the basis of what he has shown of himself in the picture

If you wish to extend the group meeting time for the retreat, or if your group is small and you move through the tasks in less time than a larger group would, you may wish to add this supplement to the *Who Am I?* exercise.

Using the *Who Am I?* drawings as the base, have each person in the group make some addition to the drawing of the other persons in the group. In his drawing or symbols he will in some way try to show something which he especially values in the person on whose picture he is drawing, or will be giving an imaginary gift to him. After each person has drawn something on every other person's drawing, have the group focus on one drawing at a time, sharing explanations of what has been added to each picture.

Before proceeding to the next drawing, have the person who has received these additions to his drawing respond by sharing how he feels about what the others have added.

RETREAT: SEGMENT FOUR

If this segment begins a new day of meeting together as a small group, use *Where I Am* as described on page 24 to begin the day together and get in touch with what is going on with each person. The exercise, *What I Need in a Partner,* which is included in this section, is to help the group to establish subgroups of from 3 to 4 persons—in the event you wish to have established groups for the subgroup work which will be done in Sessions 1, 2, 8, and 9.

Daydreaming About Relationships

PURPOSE: to have each person explore his possible ways of reaching out to a person in emotional stress

This experience is designed to help people look at their responses to other persons who need help. This will be done through the use of an imaginary situation. Invite the group to make themselves comfortable and close their eyes while you lead them through the situation. You might help the group get into the spirit for an imaginary situation if you have them sit in a circle facing one another, or with their backs all turned in to the center of the circle, or lying in a circle with their heads toward the center.

Narrate the imaginary situation slowly, reflectively, giving them plenty of time to carry out in their imagination what you suggest:

Close your eyes and get comfortable. Relax. Now imagine yourself walking down a familiar street in your town. There are houses on both sides of the street. It's a beautiful day, and you are really feeling good. As you walk along, you notice that there's a woman ahead, just sitting. You don't think much of it and continue along your way. As you draw closer, you notice that she is rather shabbily dressed and she is kind of hunched over. When you are almost up to her you notice that she is shaking with violent sobbing. She doesn't see you or seem to notice you in any way.

Now you imagine what happens next. When you do it, notice what you are feeling, what you are thinking, *and* what you did. *When you are finished, open your eyes.*

When all have finished their imaginary situations, invite them to talk about what happened in their own experience as they finished it. One at a time, each person can describe what he felt, thought, and did.

Now discuss the reactions they had. What would they like to have done differently? Might they have responded differently if the person had been a small child? An old man? An attractive member of the opposite sex? How would they feel if they had been the person crying and someone had responded to them as they did in their imaginary situation?

If you wish to extend this experience, follow this with:

Role Play of the Imaginary Situation

The group members form pairs. Each pair acts out for themselves a situation similar to the one in the imaginary situation, alternating with a woman, a man, a young child, depending on the responses they wish to explore in themselves. They might try out different ways of responding to explore the possibility of changing the way they respond, if they choose to do so.

What I Need in a Partner

PURPOSE: to enable each person to assess his own strengths and needs in a small group sharing situation

to provide data for establishing small groupings based on mutual need-meeting

Explain that during some of the sessions following the retreat, some of the exercises that the group does will occur in a subgroup of not more than four people. The subgroups will be working to help one another as they explore some of the information they build about themselves in these sessions. The work done in sub-groups will be done independently, so each group will need to provide their own leadership and support of one another as they carry out their tasks.

Suggest that, focusing on one person at a time in the group, each member list what he thinks he can offer to a small group. Some abilities persons might have to offer are: to listen, to generate new ideas, to concentrate on the task, to support others, to be enthusiastic, to organize. After he has listed his strengths, the focus person could also list what he thinks he needs from others in a group to help him work best.

As he lists these things, another person should be writing them on a sheet of newsprint, labeled with the focus person's name, and two columns headed "Abilities" and "Needs." After each person has shared both his abilities and his needs, the group can use the lists they have developed to sort themselves into appropriately-matched working groups of four persons.

The new subgroups could meet for just a few minutes. Ask each person in turn to tell the other three in his subgroup how he thinks each member of the group will be able to make his experience richer as they work together in the future.

Closing Discussions

PURPOSE: to make arrangements for time and meeting place for subsequent sessions

to end the retreat

Take this time to set a place and a time for the next meeting. This is a good time to do it, while everyone is there to mesh schedules.

Close your group meetings by talking around the group about how each person feels now that the retreat is over.

SESSION 1: EXPLORING MEANINGFUL RELATIONSHIPS—I

Where I Am

PURPOSE: to re-establish contact after a period of separation

to help each to know how the others are feeling

to give each a feeling based on awareness of themselves and others as a pattern for continuing interaction in the group

Sharing *Where I Am* was done several times on the retreat and can be used to begin each weekly session of the group. As leader, you may go first, or you could ask one of the group members to begin. In just a word or a couple of sentences each person shares how he is feeling right now and in a general way what he thinks is causing those feelings. When it seems appropriate or necessary, offer a few words of support, or reflect the feeling of members who appear to be particularly stressed.

Mini-Lecture: Talking About Ourselves

PURPOSE: to increase understanding of a purpose and use of mutual self-disclosure

This mini-lecture is best presented when the leader is talking about the content in a conversational, emotionally involved way. Underlining key phrases and using these as a guide for your presentation is one way of doing this. Here is a verbatim account of how it might be said:

We strengthen our relationships by increasing the understanding we have for one another. One important way of doing this is by sharing what we feel with each other.

When I am willing to let you know me better, I will tell you things that I ordinarily might not mention in a conversation. This involves more often telling what I am really thinking or feeling. If I feel lousy, but don't want to talk about it, and

39

you ask me how I am, I would be more honest to respond, "I would rather not talk about it right now." If you can be accepting of this, we've made a step toward greater acceptance and understanding between us at this point. My willingness to be more honest and your willingness to accept my honest self-disclosure gives us both a more solid basis for knowing some of what is going on between us.

So, sharing what I feel or what is happening to me right now is an important way of increasing understanding between us. But it's not enough if I only share my feelings honestly. I also need to learn to know and share the feelings and meanings you have in your life. If I can sense better what you are really thinking or feeling, we can know one another better. When you learn that I can know and accept what you share with me, we have a basis for sharing and trusting each other as persons.

Self-disclosure is an important key in all this. I reveal myself to you. You reveal yourself to me in whatever degree we are comfortable with. As each of us shares, we strengthen our relationship through greater understanding.

Then we can bring some of this same sharing to other relationships, and each of our lives is made richer through what we give and receive in a new relationship. This is the kind of sharing-friendship cycle we would like to start through our group.

Mini-Lecture: Really Listening

PURPOSE: to provide a cue to members as they begin initial efforts at listening with greater sensitivity to others in the group

Explain to the group that in the following exercise and during the next session, they can be helpful to one another by listening sensitively to what the other persons in their group are saying. Here is a verbatim account of how you might talk about the importance of listening:

In order to really share and understand what another person is experiencing or trying to tell you, you need to be able to sense what he is saying beyond his words. You can learn to be increasingly more sensitive to

- *the words he is saying and how he is saying them*
- *feelings implied behind his words*
- *his facial expressions, use of hands and body.*

Really listening is something you can do as others in your group share relationships which they have found good. It's something we'd like to make a part of our way of relating to each other, so it becomes a natural and habitual way of responding when other people talk. Try to provide a caring listening for one another now as you work on your relationship surveys.

Relationship Survey

PURPOSE: to increase awareness of meaningful relationships

to begin to identify qualities most valued in relationships

to continue experience in shared self-disclosure

to provide opportunity for listening in a caring way

Materials needed will be brush pens and sheets of newsprint. Group members will work in the subgroups they organized during the retreat, or, if they did not organize these, have them divide into groups of 3 or 4.

Explain to the group that now you'll all be thinking and talking about relationships that have been especially important to you at some time in your lives. This will be done by working out what is called a relationship survey on each one of you. In order to show what it is like, you as leader can demonstrate by doing yours for the group and going through the entire experience with them.

Tape up a sheet of newsprint, write your name on it, and divide the top two-thirds into two columns. In the first column write the names of four persons with whom you have had relationships that you have valued greatly. These may be relationships from the present and from the past. After each person's name write what it is that you value in the relationship.

As you write out your sheet, talk about the relationships as openly as you can to help others also feel comfortable about sharing relationships which have been meaningful to them. When you have completed the list, the other members of the group can respond to your sharing by thinking through what you have said and written. Then they can identify:

"Your more meaningful relationships seem to happen when _____, or with people who _____."

Have someone summarize what the group says on the bottom third of your newsprint sheet. List out the observations the members make. For example:

Relationships that are important to you are ones in which

- you experience warmth from others
- you are being taken care of
- you feel important

When members have shared their ideas on what seems to characterize your more meaningful relationships, you tell them how you felt about the experience.

After you have carried out your relationship survey in the total group, the subgroups can meet in separate rooms and take turns sharing this information for themselves among members of the subgroup. Time this next session carefully, and stop the group about 35 minutes before closing time to carry out the rest of the session. The groups will finish their surveys during the second weekly session.

Announcements
Take some time to make plans for meeting places, hand out any materials you have, make any other announcements.

Next time you will need a meeting place where you can meet in small groups and then gather in a room large enough to post all the relationship surveys on the wall. Collect the relationship surveys so you can use them again next week.

Goal Setting

PURPOSE: to acquaint members with the goal-setting principles

to do goal setting for the coming week

It is important that you do a thorough job of presentation on goals this first night. This will set the stage for a pattern of goal setting which the group will follow during each of the remaining sessions. Help your group members select goals within the guidelines, as this will give them a greater assurance of a successful outcome. During this first session, the group may find it easiest to set goals related to things or tasks such as

- make a birthday cake
- finish my overdue book report
- clean my closet

Later they may choose to set goals related to other people or to their relationships with other people. However, relationship goals are sometimes more difficult to set in a way which provides a clear sense of accomplishment, so it is recommended that they begin with non-people goals.

Here is the primary information that should be conveyed about goal setting:

Goal setting is a way to get things done, to change, to become the kind of person you want to be. Each week we will be setting goals and sharing our results with other group members. It works like this:

- *You select a goal you want to reach.*
- *You act—carry out your goal.*
- *You experience the satisfaction of completing your goal.*
- *This encourages you to set another.*
- *You act—carry out this goal.*

- *So the cycle goes on, to a greater sense of satisfaction and achievement.*

Here are some guidelines for setting goals. Goals should be:

Conceivable: capable of being put into words

Believable: acceptable as appropriate to your values

Achievable: can be accomplished with your present strengths

Controllable: does not depend upon a specific response from another person in order to achieve it

Measurable: you can observe it, you can count it

Desirable: something you really want to do

Stated with no alternatives: not optional, and one at a time

Growth facilitating: not injurious to self, others, society

When we follow these guidelines, we have a better chance of completing a goal successfully.

After the idea of goal setting has been discussed, the leader can start the group by setting his goal first. Then, as each member of the group chooses a goal, he can tell it to the group. Try to keep the goal setting moving along fairly quickly, but check on each goal to see that it meets the guidelines for goal setting.

Closing
PURPOSE: to give a sense of completeness to the meeting

Each group has its own style and needs in closing a meeting. A group song, a big hug, or just saying goodnight may be what suits this group. Discuss with the group how they would like to feel when they leave the meeting and what would help them to feel that way. Then select your own activity and style for closing.

SESSION 2: EXPLORING MEANINGFUL RELATIONSHIPS—II

Where I Am
Repeat this experience as described in Session 1.

Relationship Survey
PURPOSE: to increase awareness of meaningful relationships

to begin to identify qualities most valued in relationships

to continue experience in giving and receiving self-disclosure

to provide opportunity for listening in a caring way

The group began sharing their Relationship Surveys in their subgroups last week. Pass these out to them again and suggest that they continue this work in their subgroups until each person in the group has finished his. If they need a reminder of what the task was, refer back to Session 1 and repeat the instructions. In summary:

- One member lists significant relationships and what is important about each relationship.
- Other members react to what he says by trying to help him identify what characterizes relationships which are most meaningful to him.
- The person who has talked about his relationships tells the group how he feels about this experience.

Group Summary of Relationship Surveys
PURPOSE: to summarize the survey experience

to look for specific insights and common characteristics among the participants

When all of the subgroups have completed their sharing, have each person post his newsprint sheet on the wall so that all sheets can be seen at once. The total group will participate in this next part.

When all the surveys have been posted, take some time for everyone to look over the surveys. Ask each person to think over what he learned about himself and write this on his sheet. When everyone has completed this kind of browsing and summarizing, spend some time in the total group discussing what they discovered. If their discussion does not include attempts at summarizing the sheets, you might ask for some summarizing observations.

Mini-Lecture: Trust

PURPOSE: to provide a conceptual framework for understanding the increasing trust levels in the group

to provide an understanding from which some kinds of responses of fear and uncertainty can be more easily accepted

Here is a verbatim account of the kind of ideas you may communicate about trust:

An important thing that is happening in our group is that we are beginning to build feelings of trust for one another. Trusting each other is the kind of thing that makes it feel a little safer to

- *dare to show more of what I am*
- *dare to share more of the parts of me that I don't feel so good about, or the parts that feel very special.*

When I trust you, it is a little easier to do things that I might be afraid to do otherwise, like showing affection, or like doing nutty things that I could be afraid you wouldn't like.

Sometimes we may feel a little uneasy about this kind of openness among us. That's what makes the trusting so important, because, in the face of feeling a little new or uneasy at this, we can gradually learn to do the things we want to do with one another, at our own pace.

When we trust each other, we feel safer to be whatever we feel like being just at that moment. We can take off our masks, our pretensions, and just be people—and change and grow together.

Announcements

Set meeting time, place, and cover any other business needing attention in the group.

Goal Reporting

PURPOSE: to begin to establish a pattern of conscious goal selection and achievement

to reinforce successful goal fulfillment by sharing with other group members

The pattern of setting goals and reporting them will be repeated each week. The group will report on the goals they set from the week before and then set new goals for the coming week. Take this time for each member to report how his experience went with meeting his goal for this week. Keep the conversation from drifting to other topics and give each person adequate time to talk about the outcome of his effort to reach his goal. If a person failed to fulfill his goal, accept his explanation, and then later make a special effort to check his goal setting for the next week to help assure him that the same thing won't happen the following week.

Goal Setting

PURPOSE: to follow up the goal reporting with a new round of goal setting to help strengthen a pattern of success in meeting goals

Point out that this is the second round with goal setting and that each week will provide an opportunity for a new round of goals. It is more important to select goals they want and feel they can reasonably meet than to select large, difficult-to-meet goals time after time. Goals which are very difficult can become a burden and slow down goal-meeting behavior.

If the members feel willing to do so, they may wish to focus their goal setting on some factor related to the PEER plan so far, such as:

• Listen more carefully to what other people say.

• Learn more about how others feel by noticing the way they act (observe your English teacher before class each day and write

49

down how he/she seems to be feeling, or your mother in the morning before school, or your friend).

- Count the number of times you sense that someone around you is especially troubled by something during this week.

Encourage group members to pick a goal they will enjoy meeting and which will help them to grow in some way. As each person selects his goal, invite the group to check to see if it meets the guidelines for maximizing success.

Closing
Choose how you and your group wish to close, and do it.

SESSION 3: IDENTIFYING MY STRENGTHS

Where I Am
Repeat this experience as described in Session 1.

Strength Bombardment
PURPOSE: to provide information about the positive impressions others have of us

to help participants see themselves in a more positive way

to give experience in disclosure of positive feelings toward others

to give experience in receiving and accepting positive feedback from others

By way of introduction, you can point out that in the relationship surveys you were identifying what you value in other relationships. This exercise is an opportunity to identify things you value in one another. There are two alternative ways of doing strength bombardment presented here. The first method is less demanding on each individual member of the group and provides greater group support and participation. The second provides a greater personal encounter and sharing between each individual member with every other individual member, and tends to require greater poise. You may wish to do either one, or both.

First Method
The group sits in a circle. One person is selected for strength bombardment and is given a paper and pencil. Then the other members of the group identify the personal strengths they see in this person—especially strengths which they value in a relationship. As the group mentions these strengths, the person being bombarded writes down the characteristics they mention. After a number of strengths have been mentioned, or the group slows down in their identification of strengths, ask the person being bombarded to read the list of things that have been said about him. After he has read the list, he can tell the group how he feels about what they have told him.

Each person in the group gets a turn until all members of the group have been given the strength bombardment.

Second Method
Give each person a small pad of paper and a pencil. Each person will mill around the room, and one by one, meet with the other members of the group. When persons stop to talk to one another, they will identify what they see as the greatest single strength in the other person. Then they write this on the small pad of paper and tape that paper with the strength written on it (1) on the person being identified as having the strength, or (2) on that person's Relationship Survey which is posted on the wall in the room in which you are meeting. Whenever two persons identify strengths in one another, they should try to be open to really "hearing" their partner's positive feelings about them.

Ask the group members to sit on the floor when they have named a strength for each member of the group so you can know when they're done. When everyone is through, gather the group together for discussion. How did this experience feel for each person there? Was it difficult to receive the positive comments openly without denying the strength or apologizing for oneself? What was it like to tell other people what you like about them? What did you learn in this experience?

Mini-Lecture: Your Perception of Me
Purpose: to call attention to the importance of the way we perceive and act toward other people

This summary discusses some effects of the way people view one another:
If you think of me as being a person who has certain limitations or specific traits, and you hold this as a fixed perception of me, you will tend to discourage or fail to recognize other attributes of my personality. In your presence, I will be less likely to reach beyond what you now see as my being—into new growth and possibility.

But if you also see within me the potential, the promise of change—and act toward me as though this is possible—this will help me to change more readily. Your expectations of me become a part of how I see myself and the world around me, and they have a tendency to become realized.

This is called self-fulfilling prophecy. Because of the influence you have in my life in this way, I need you to be a friend who thinks well of me, who believes in my capacity to respond adequately to difficulty, and who is willing to see me change and seek out my own way of living fully—my own way of being my own kind of person.

Announcements

Set meeting time and place for the next meeting. Include any other announcements.

Save the lists of strengths which are developed for each person in some form so they can be read again next week.

Goal Reporting and Goal Setting

PURPOSE: to establish a pattern of conscious goal selection and achievement

to reinforce successful goal fulfillment by sharing with other group members

Some of the members may wish to begin setting goals which focus on relationships. These goals are somewhat more complex than other goals because in order to feel successful, the goal setter needs to feel he has accomplished his goal, regardless of what the response of the other person is.

Example: If your goal is to serve breakfast in bed to your mother, can you feel good about accomplishing the goal regardless of your mother's response? In the rare instance that she may not appreciate it, you have been successful in completing your goal, because you *did* it.

In this example your success is not based on how your mother felt about what you did. This is *uncontrollable* according to the guidelines. Serving breakfast, you can control; your mother's response, you can't control. Try to hang your sense of accomplishment on the completion of the relationship act and not the response of the person you are relating to. Point this out to the group members so they can set goals on relationships with this in mind.

Have the group divide into small groups of three persons each. Within the small groups each person can talk about how things went for them in meeting their goals for this week. When they have finished talking about the goal of the past week, they can select another goal for the coming week. Remind them to check each other out to make sure they are following the guidelines for goal setting.

Closing
Do your group's favorite thing, or look for a new one.

SESSION 4: USING MY STRENGTHS

Where I Am
Repeat this experience as described in Session 1.

Using My Strengths
PURPOSE: to encourage thinking of ourselves as growing and changing

to identify obstacles in present behavior which prevent us from making maximum use of our strengths

Display the lists of strengths in some way so they can each be read, or have them on hand so they can be referred to as each person becomes a center of focus. One by one each person in the group will take a turn to be the center of attention for this exercise.

Select one person to begin. First, ask him to read, or you read for him, the list of strengths that was generated for him during the last session. After his strengths have been reviewed, he should turn to the group and ask them:

What do you see in me that gets in the way of my using my strengths most fully?

The group will respond by mentioning things which they feel may make a difference in enabling him to maximize his strengths more fully. If this portion of the sharing begins to look like a "slam" session, remind them they are identifying factors which will help this person *heighten the use of his strengths*. Focus the attention on what gets in the way of his using his strengths most fully, *not* on what's wrong with him.

Not everyone will contribute in this discussion. In some cases it is possible there will be no response at all. If so, don't push it. When the group has described one or more things which may be getting

59

in the focus person's way of using his strengths most fully, invite them to do an imaginary situation for this person.

For the situation, each person in the group lets his imagination run to what might possibly become of this person *if he used his strengths most fully.* The fantasy focuses on the good, or exciting, or fulfilling things which conceivably could happen, given the use of his strengths, 5 to 10 years into the future. Encourage the group to let their imaginations run wild. Sometimes the most far-out fantasies are the most helpful to the person receiving them.

Invite the group to talk about the fantasies they have for this person. Not all persons will have fantasies for each person in the group. Several fantasies for each person may be enough depending on how prolifically your group is generating them.

After sharing the fantasies, ask the person being focused on to talk about his feelings in reaction to the experience.

Move on to the next person, until each person in the group has had a turn.

For your convenience in repeated use of the sequence, the steps are:

- Review strengths from the last meeting.
- Ask group what gets in the way of using strengths most fully.
- Fantasize about next 5 to 10 years if strengths are used fully.
- Person focused on shares his reaction to the experience.

Mini-Lecture: Self-Perception and Relationships

PURPOSE: to increase awareness of how self-perception affects the way people act and influences the way others respond to them

Here is a verbatim account of some ideas you can communicate on influences of self-perception:

The way I think of myself is very important in affecting what I am like when I am with others. The way they think of themselves is very important in determining what they are like when they are with me. If I think of myself as someone who is likable and capable, I will be more likely to be friendly to other people, and confident in approaching them. The more I act like a likable person, the more other people will think of me as being likable, and in our relationship we will rediscover the goodness of who we are.

On the other hand, if I think of myself as being undesirable in some way, I will probably hold back in relationships. I will assume that others do not want me. When they sense me holding back, they will probably leave me alone or let me drop out. Now I am living as though I am undesirable, because I feel that way and show it in the way I act.

But there is another part to this. When I sense that other people really like me, that they believe in my ability to do something, this helps me believe in myself, and I begin to act more the way they expect me to act.

I can help them feel good about themselves in the same way by communicating my liking for them and my trust in them.

So, the way I think of myself helps me to be what I am. This is also true of other people. The way they think of themselves and the way I think of myself affects what happens between us.

Announcements
Set meeting time and place. Make any other announcements needed.

Goal Reporting and Goal Setting
PURPOSE: to establish a pattern of conscious goal selection and achievement

to reinforce successful goal fulfillment by sharing with other group members

to do goal setting with a new twist

61

Ask the group members to meet in the same groups of three in which they set goals last week. They should each tell how their goal went and identify what they might have done differently if their achievement was not satisfactory to them. After each person has reported on his last week's goal, the group will work to build goals for the next week. This time have them write down their goal on a 3x5 card. It is not necessary to put their name on the card. Ask them to hand the completed card in to the leader when their goals have been set.

Closing

You might select a closing which fits with the theme for the evening in some way.

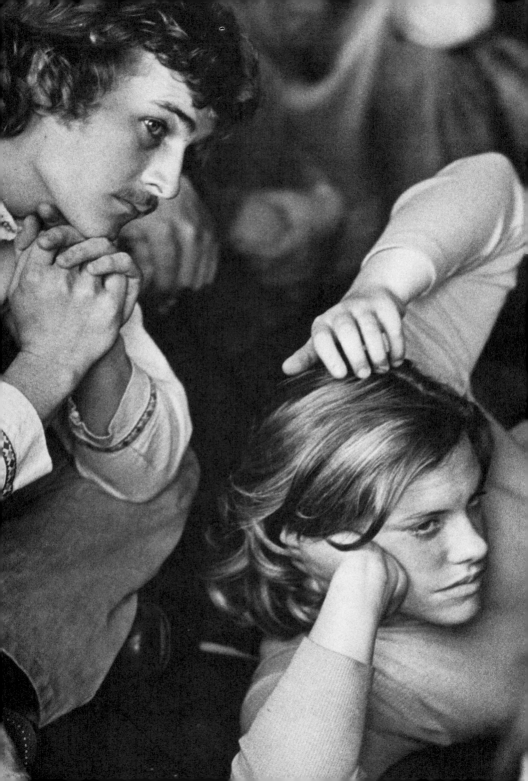

SESSION 5: LEARNING TO LISTEN

Where I Am
Repeat this experience as described in Session 1.

Sharing Something Important
PURPOSE: to provide a base sharing experience between two people before learning special communication skills

During the next few sessions we will be focusing much attention on communication skills. This initial sharing experience will help to provide a baseline for what will be following.

Ask each person in the group to find a partner—someone they haven't seen much of lately. Each person in the pair will have about five minutes to tell his partner about something that has been very important to him lately. This could be something very exciting, or troubling, but something that he has strong feelings about.

When the time is up, call the group together again and move on to the mini-lecture. The group will discuss this experience at the end of the session.

Mini-Lecture: Introduction to Reflective Listening
PURPOSE: to provide a context for trying reflective listening

to describe conceptually what reflective listening is

Before you present this material to the group it is important for you to really *know* and *understand* it.

This is a verbatim demonstration of what might be said to teach the concept of reflective listening:

Throughout this series we have been working on learning to be more understanding and accepting of others in our relationships.

We have been experiencing more and more understanding and acceptance. Now we would like to turn our attention to learning the communication skills that make it possible to talk directly about the understanding we are reaching for.

Suppose you are talking with a person who has a lot of feelings. Maybe he is upset about something—or feels especially good. How can he know that you understand what he is saying? How can you communicate acceptance of what he is saying so he will feel encouraged to continue to share with you? You can do it through reflective listening, *which looks like this:*

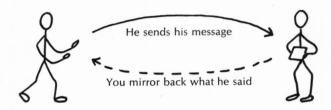

He sends his message

You mirror back what he said

Your friend has expressed his feelings, or described something to you. To make sure you understand him, or to show your acceptance of what you understand him to say, you say to him, in different words, what you understand him to mean. *You provide a kind of mirror or reflection of what he is saying.*

If he says, "I'm so sick I can hardly stand up," you might respond, "Wow, you're really feeling rotten." If he says, "Hey, guess what! I made the first team in swimming!" You might say, "The first team! You really sound excited."

The main thing you want to hear and respond to when people share in this way is their feeling. If your response can pick up and reflect feelings, you are closer to what is going on inside the other person, and your communication is more true and more close to what's really happening. Sometimes what you feed back to the other person is a kind of summarizing, like, "So the teacher blamed you for something Tom did, and now you've been criticized and you don't want to tell her what really happened because you don't want to sell out on Tom." Sometimes this is also very helpful in communicating understanding and helping the other person clarify his own situation. The important key in reflective listening is to listen as accurately as possible to what the other person is saying—and to send this meaning back to him in different words. Your response is based on the other person's feelings. Your goal is to be in touch with what is happening inside him.

Demonstration of Reflective Listening

PURPOSE: to provide a model to demonstrate reflective listening

Ask a volunteer from the group to think of some problem he has right now—perhaps a teacher he is having trouble with, or a friend who irritates him, or a decision he has to make. Ask him to tell the group about it, and let them respond in whatever ways seem natural to them. Ask the problem-sharer to stop talking after each sentence or two, so that the group has time to respond.

Now ask the problem-sharer to begin again, and tell the same problem to the leader, while the group merely listens. This time, the leader tries to reflect the feelings and/or content of what the sharer is saying.

Discuss what different things happened in the two situations. Were the two conversations different in tone? Were they different in what subjects were discussed, or how they were discussed? How does the problem-sharer feel about the two conversations? If it seems useful, you might try the same exercise again with a different problem-sharer, and a different problem.

Mini-Lecture: Being Less Helpful Than We Thought

PURPOSE: to identify a few common responses which a listener may make in an effort to be helpful, but which have the opposite effect

Here is a verbatim summary of what might be said:

Sometimes when we are talking with another person and we are trying to be helpful, we say the kinds of things that have been

said to us all our lives. Our intentions may be good, but often these "helpful" things get in the way more than they help. Here are some:

> *Probing and asking questions. This throws the speaker off the track of his own thinking, so he really is not sharing in his own way any longer. Sometimes questions seem snoopy, or imply that the speaker has made a mistake, or that the questioner wants to take off in a different direction.*

> *Giving advice, or trying to push a person into what you think is the "right" way. Often this feels pushy, and suggests that the advice-giver won't be happy until the other person comes across and does things his way. It also suggests that the advice-giver thinks he knows all the answers and is superior.*

As a helping person, try to avoid doing these things. They often work against greater understanding and sharing. Your strength lies in being a friend and "being there" when a friend is needed. When you try to do these other things (questioning, giving advice) you increase the possibility of making communication more difficult, and turning your friend away.

Trying It With the Man in the Flying Machine

PURPOSE: to give participants an initial trial at using reflective listening responses

As the leader, you will take the part of the man with the problem during this exercise. The members of your group will be your good friend with whom you are having a cup of coffee. You will share your problems with them, with as much real feeling as you think such a man would have. When you play the role, say the name of the person that you want to respond with a reflective statement, moving to a different one for each statement. Stay in the role as much as possible so the group can more readily pick up on your feeling. You may need to coach some members by saying,

68

"Stick with my feeling," "Try to say back to me what you hear me saying, only using different words."

I'm glad you could meet me for coffee. I've really been needing someone to talk to. I've really been feeling rotten the last couple days.

Lately a funny thing has been happening; my eyes were kind of bothering me. Everytime I read much I'd get these headaches.

Finally I figured I'd better check it out with the doctor, and boy, I was really in for a shock.

After the doc had me all checked over, he tells me I've got to have new glasses.

Well, you know, that happens to everyone, so at first I didn't think too much about it. Then he started telling me about some limitations I'd have and that was where I really got hit with it.

It seems the glasses I need are the type that are below government minimum standards for vision, and I can't be licensed to fly anymore.

It's really tough for pilots, almost like dying a little.

Flying is the big love of my life. I've done it for years. It's the greatest feeling I know to be way up there soaring. The freedom just takes over and you really feel great.

Whenever things were down, I could always count on a few hours of flying to make me feel better again.

Then there were so many great times we had. The whole family would take off for Canada to go fishing, or I'd go hunting in Wyoming with the guys. We'd just load up and take off. It was a tremendous feeling of freedom and adventure.

The kids are really excited about flying. They really feel let down if I take off for a weekend without them.

My wife isn't as fond of it as they are, though.

She's a little afraid of flying. She's always reading these stories

69

about crashes in small planes, and she worries a lot, especially when I take the kids up.

We do have some good times together, though, when we go on the trips with the whole family.

We had talked about doing a lot more camping—possibly buying a cabin in the woods somewhere, but I haven't had a lot of time, and I've been doing a lot of flying.

Well, no more flying now. No more soaring in the clouds, that's over. And I really enjoyed it.

Guess I could find some other ways to enjoy life. There are a lot of things I've always wanted to do that I've never taken time for.

Maybe I could spend some of that old flying time on some outings with the family. We could buy a cabin, explore the woods, maybe get a boat and do some fishing right where our cabin is.

Thanks for meeting me. It's been good to have someone to talk to about this.

I feel better already.

Discussion of Reflective Listening
PURPOSE: to give group members an opportunity to share their reactions and questions after their first attempt at reflective listening

Invite the group to give their reaction to trying to do reflective listening. Avoid trying to convince people who may question its usefulness. Instead, try reflecting their feelings.

Mini-Lecture: Guidelines for Reflective Listening
PURPOSE: to provide some guidelines on how to make reflective listening more effective

Here is a verbatim presentation of some ideas to communicate to the group. It is helpful to write these out on newsprint and post them.

70

Here are some guidelines which may be helpful to you as you learn to do reflective listening. In reflective listening:

- *Say the same thing in a different way, with different words, or reflect how you perceive him to be feeling.*
- *Stick with where the person is. Don't lag behind, or go farther than he has already suggested.*
- *Speak with the same feeling he has; feel it with him.*
- *Use reflective listening only when you can feel accepting of the other person.*

Use reflective listening when

- *the other person*
  talks about or expresses feelings (sometimes nonverbally)
  has a problem
  is sharing ideas which are important to him
  is angry, assaultive, resistant
- *or when you*
  are unsure what the other person means
  think you understand and want to check it out
  want to "share" or be with the other person.

When you listen, you are saying to the other person:
"You are important. I want to understand you."

Something Important Revisited

PURPOSE: to provide more experience in reflective listening, this time with a real situation

to contrast reflective listening with usual communication patterns

Invite the pairs who first met at the beginning of the meeting to get together again, to talk about the same thing, but this time with a difference. This time, ask those who are listening to respond with reflective listening. Give each pair fifteen minutes to do this sharing. After the practice is completed, call the group together and discuss how it went, what went well, what may have felt uncomfortable.

Announcements

Set meeting place and time for the next meeting. Make any other announcements or arrangements needed.

Goal Reporting and Setting

PURPOSE: to establish a pattern of conscious goal selection and achievement

to reinforce successful goal fulfillment by sharing with other group members

Last week each member filled out a 3x5 card listing what his goal is. This week, pass these cards out at random. Then one by one, have the group members read the goal written on the card. When the goal is read, the person who wrote that goal will identify it as his goal, and talk briefly about how he met that goal. When each goal has been reported on, ask the group if this week they would be willing to make a goal to use reflective listening in some situation. If some prefer not to, they can set a goal on some other item they are interested in. For those doing goals in reflective listening, ask each person to tell the group in what situation they plan to try it during the coming week.

Closing

SESSION 6: COMMUNICATING YOUR OWN FEELING

Where I Am

Repeat this experience as described in Session 1.

Goal Reporting

PURPOSE: to provide an opportunity to report on experience in using reflective listening before review of the skill

One variation of this exercise is to ask people to talk about their reflective listening experience when they share in the *Where I Am* experience at the beginning. Another way is to ask each person to find one or two other people and to share what his experience was in using reflective listening during the week.

Discussion About Reflective Listening

PURPOSE: to clarify any questions about reflective listening which have cropped up during their attempts to use it

When the groups have shared their experiences with the goals of the past week, check to see if they have any questions of discomfort in the use of reflective listening. Discuss these briefly, then move into the next exercise.

Listening with One Another

PURPOSE: to provide greater familiarity and practice in using reflective listening

Ask the members of the group to think of some experience they have had during the past week which they have some strong feelings about—happiness, anger, frustration, pleasure. Ask them to find a partner they would like to talk to about this. Each partner will listen to the other as he shares his experience or feelings of the past week. Give the group 20 minutes to complete this, and tell them when 10 minutes are up so they can shift, and the other of the pair can respond with reflective listening.

When the time is up, invite the group to discuss their reactions to the experience. During the ensuing discussion some people will probably mention that reflective listening seems incomplete as an option in conversation because it doesn't seem to provide any input. This observation can be used as a jumping off point for instruction about the "I" message.

Mini-Lecture: Communicating Your Own Feeling

PURPOSE: to tie the "I" message in with reflective listening

to provide a conceptual basis for understanding and using the "I" message

The following provides a verbatim description of how this information may be communicated:

As you have been using reflective listening so far, you may have felt that at times it doesn't seem to be enough to complete a transaction. When we take a look at reflective listening we can see that it focuses on the relationship from one side—sharing and understanding from the point of view of the speaker. Reflective listening communicates that the speaker is being listened to and understood. But still only one person is being heard. (Use reflective listening diagram from last week to demonstrate if this is helpful.)

Reflective listening is a very important skill, and often it is complete by itself, but it is not complete as a communication of a relationship. A full relationship is a reciprocal process. So we need to learn how to share ourselves as well as to listen.

When I am sharing my own feelings, the focus is on me. When I speak this way it is called an "I" message. There are several pieces of information that are really important to the person I am talking to. They are shown on this chart:

76

| What has happened | How I feel | How this affects me (This is sometimes hard to say, but do so whenever you can.) |

"I" messages may communicate either positive or negative feelings. Let's try one now and see how it goes.

Demonstration of an "I" Message

Pick out someone from your group and do something to them which will get a strong reaction—preferably negative for this phase of learning. For example, go over and break someone's wooden pencil.

Your Comments	*Their Response*
What happened?	You broke my pencil.
How do you feel?	I'm hurt and confused.
How does this affect you?	I'll have to buy another pencil.

As soon as this transaction is completed, immediately respond to the person about their "I" message by reacting as you usually would if spoken to that way such as,

I'm really sorry you feel bad.
I was just trying to demonstrate an "I" message.
I hope you won't be mad at me.

Now ask him to reflect your response

So you don't want me to feel irritated with you.

Now you describe the transaction you just completed.

You just gave me an "I" message. You told me what happened, how you feel about it and how it affects you.

Point out to the group that reflective listening is an important follow through for a negative "I" message. If you come out with a strong negative "I" message, the person you are being honest with in this way will probably feel hurt or defensive at first.

77

It is important to listen reflectively to their response immediately after you have given them the "I" message. A guideline is to give an "I" message, and then reflect the other person's response.

Practice Doing An "I" Message

Divide the group into small groups of three to practice doing "I" messages. In this grouping, two people in the group will carry out the transaction and the third person will watch and coach to help them do it. Then the three persons will change roles in the group until every person has had a try at giving an "I" message.

Post a newsprint sheet with this sequence drawn on it to help demonstrate the interaction they are to have.

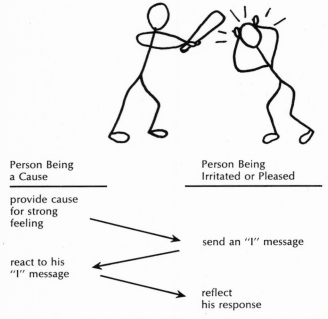

Person Being
a Cause

Person Being
Irritated or Pleased

provide cause
for strong
feeling

              send an "I" message

react to his
"I" message

              reflect
his response

Take one of the groups of three and use them to demonstrate the kinds of transactions they are to have. You coach, and this provides them with additional examples for what they are to do.

78

After this learning task is completed, invite the group members to share their reactions. This will give you a better idea of what they are learning and where they are having difficulty.

Mini-Lecture: When to Use "I" Messages
PURPOSE: to identify appropriate use of "I" messages

Here is an account of information to provide about "I" messages:
The "I" message is a way of sharing what is going on in you. It can tell other people the effect they have on us. Sometimes a good "I" message will change the way other people act.

Send "I" messages when the other person
- *is a problem to you in some way*
- *seems unclear about what you are trying to communicate or when you*
  - *are inclined to give advice, criticize, or preach and you may come across as wanting to "win" or as someone who thinks he has the right answer*
  - *have been using reflective listening and now want or need to tell what's going on inside you*
  - *have an experience or feeling you want to share.*

If you are reflective listening and you feel a strong stirring or restlessness inside you, that may be a signal that you have some feelings that could be shared. You may need to send an "I" message, or you may be unable to continue listening authentically.

"I" messages about the positive things you experience with other people can multiply good feelings. Practice sending these, too.

When sending "I" messages be sure to send all your feelings. If you send only half, your message might not come across straight.

Here, it is so important to be open and honest. Being a real person, sharing yourself with another person, is the key.

79

When you share yourself through an "I" message, you are telling the other person:

> *My needs are important. I would like you to know me. I will let you know me.*

Mini-Lecture: How to Do Role Play

PURPOSE: to prepare the group for participating in role-play situations

Here is a description of how you might orient your group to the role-play situation in which they will be polishing their reflective listening skills.

During the next few sessions we will be using role-play situations to help us experience some of the kinds of situations we may encounter as we reach out in new relationships.

There are two general kinds of things we can learn when we do role-play

- *We can get a better sense for how another person may feel when we play his role; what it's like to be on drugs, pregnant, lonely, etc.*

- *We can practice our skills and be better prepared to respond comfortably when we run into situations similar to the type we work within the role play.*

When you are doing role play, you will be given only the one role to read if you are the helper. This is done so that you will be basically uninformed about the problem your friend has, and it is up to him to share his problem with you in his own way. Your job is to be a friend, using the kinds of communication skills we have learned.

The role-play situations provided give only a few brief details as a guide to what you do and say. You can fill in all the details in any way you want—talk as you think such a person would talk, or the way you would talk if you were in that situation. Try to feel as you think that person might feel, and play out the role the way you feel it. Stay in the role. Do not get into conversations about the role, nor "editorialize" to others. If you really get into it, it can be a lot of fun.

Doing a Role Play

PURPOSE: to provide experience in using active listening in situations where someone is sharing a problem

To demonstrate how the role play is done, ask for two volunteers who will try it first in the center of the circle. This will provide a practice run for both those who watch and those who demonstrate. Give one of the role situations to the volunteer pair, and then coach them as they attempt to model a problem sharing—active listening interaction. If you have ample time, model the second role-play situation in the total group also. The following week everyone will have a chance to function in the role play situation.

Role-Play Situation 1

JIM

You are a 14-year-old boy who has been feeling very lonely. You feel that your parents don't understand you, they don't hear what you try to say to them. You don't have anyone around to talk to. Your friends—the people you call your friends—don't call you. You have to contact them all the time, and you're not so sure you can really call them friends. It seems to you that people make fun of you—laugh at you. You'd really like to have someone to talk to, and you wish other people would show that they want you for a friend. But you figure that you're not worth much anyway, so no wonder people don't pay much attention to you. You'd really like someone to like you—but then maybe they can't.

Then one day you happened to have a chance to talk for a while with an older friend in your neighborhood.

FRIEND TO JIM

You live in the same neighborhood as Jim. You've noticed that he seems to be kind of a loner, and he looks kind of sad, with not much enthusiasm for anything. You've just learned about doing reflective listening. Today you are out in the yard when Jim comes by. You smile at him, and he kind of hangs around. After awhile, you start talking together.

Role-Play Situation 2
BILL

You are 15 years old. You hate school—it's really a drag. It doesn't seem to make any sense to you; you have to do so many things that just don't seem to count for much. The sooner you get out the better. It's really frustrating to have to keep at it in school when you hate it so much, and sometimes you get so mad you'd like to explode. When it comes right down to it, school is really hard work. You don't understand a lot of what your teachers want you to do, and you really feel miserable—and dumb. It's just too much, and that's why you feel you'd just as soon give up on everything.

One of your buddies has an older brother you've always liked—and he seems to like you. Today, you had a chance to talk to him for a while, and some of your feelings about school come out in your conversation.

FRIEND TO BILL

You don't know Bill well, but he pals around with your kid brother. You've always liked Bill, and sometimes you kid around with him. Your kid brother has mentioned that Bill really hates school. You've been learning some about helping out guys with some problems, and you decide to sit down with him—and try some of the reflective listening that you've been learning about, to see if you can get some better understanding of his situation. It might help if he feels that someone understands.

Announcements
Set meeting date and place and make any other announcements that are needed.

Goal Setting
PURPOSE: to establish a pattern of conscious goal selection and
achievement

Up to this time, each group member has set a series of five goals. Before setting a new goal this week, it may be valuable to review in their own minds what they have done, how it has worked out, and where they want to go from here with their goal setting. What areas do they want to strengthen themselves in? What specific kinds of goals seem to be most important to them right now? Ask them to find partners and talk this over. After they have summarized their thinking about their goal-setting experiences with their partners, they can select a new goal for the coming week.

Closing

Where I Am

Repeat this experience as described in Session 1.

Quick Review of Active Listening

PURPOSE: to provide another experience in intensive use of reflective listening responses

Explain to the group that you'll be doing quick reviews of both reflective listening and "I" messages and then focusing on some role-play situations where they will have an opportunity to use both skills.

Suggest that each person find a partner with whom he has not yet practiced reflective listening. In the pairs, spend five minutes each talking about something that happened during the week that each one has a lot of feelings about. Listening partner should do reflective listening.

Practice of "I" Messages

PURPOSE: to review the "I" message

to provide practice using an "I" message in varied situations which will arouse positive or negative responses

Give a quick review of the "I" message and the three parts:

What happened	How I feel	How this affects me

Using the *"I" Message Practice Sheet,* present these situations to members of the group and ask them to respond with the kind of "I" message they would give if they were in that situation. Coach the group members where they need it as they work to develop greater skill in communicating their feelings.

85

Point out that:

"I" messages can be used as a way of helping other people change their behavior. If they are unaware of what it is in their own behavior that tends to get them in trouble with other people, your honest response to them through a straight "I" message is one of the most effective ways of helping them to know and to change their own behavior.

"I" MESSAGE PRACTICE SHEET

What "I" messages would you send to these?

1. Your new friend seems to like going places with you. But he is always late. You have to wait at least a half hour for him every time you do something together. Often you are late getting to ball games or movies. Tonight he picks you up at your house. He is 45 minutes late.

2. You've been trying to be a friend to Sally. But she has latched on and wants to be with you all the time. You don't get the time you want to be with other friends, have time alone, and just do your own thing.

3. You've found a friend (opposite sex) whom you really would like to help and be friends with, but he/she keeps putting on a big sex come-on.

4. Your friend has been changing gradually. The clothes he wears have been getting way-out. You have noticed that you are becoming embarrassed when you go places with him.

5. You come home to find that your roommate (sister, brother) has just cleaned the room you share. He's there, and you say . . . .

6. Your friend has just called at 11:30 P.M. You were in bed sleeping. He says, "Hi, just thought I'd call and rap for a while."

7. You've been out of touch with your friend for awhile. You've really missed him—but you've been busy. Now you go to the store to pick up some things, and you run across him there.

8. You are goofing around with some kids. One of them takes some goopy stuff and drips it over your clothes.

9. You have a new friend. Today you found him/her flirting with your steady.

10. Your mom cooked a supper of some of your favorite foods.

11. You're housebound with a broken leg. Your friend gives up the ball game and dance and spends the evening keeping you company.

12. You are taking a test. Your classmate keeps trying to read your answers over your shoulder.

13. Your new friend borrowed your favorite sweater to wear to a party. When he/she returns it, it is dirty and there's a small hole in the elbow. He/she says nothing about it and acts as though nothing has happened.

Role Play: Being a Friend to Someone Who Needs You
PURPOSE: to provide concentrated experience in playing a helping or supportive role

Work in recent weeks has focused on developing communication skills which help the group members to be more understanding, show acceptance, and communicate to others where they are at in the relationship at the present time. These role-play situations provide additional experience in use of the skills.

As leader, you serve as coach to help the group members maximize their skills. It is often useful to ask the people who play the roles how they feel in response to their partner. Was the reflective listening helpful? Did they feel understood? Understanding?

Begin the role play by asking for the first one or two situations to be played out in the center of the group by two volunteers. Then when the group is comfortable with the nature of the tasks, have them break into smaller groups where all of them can get experience taking the role of a friend.

When the groups have completed the role playing, bring them back into one group and ask them to talk about how the experience went. What *felt* especially good? What *went* especially well? What are some areas in which they feel they need greater skill? Were the participants able to achieve a sense of acceptance between them? How did this feel?

Role-Play Situation 3

DONNA

You are 15 years old. You've always been a good student at school, but you haven't had a lot of friends until lately. Then you got in with a group of kids, and for the first time you feel that you have friends you can relate to and feel equal with. But this group has been using drugs more and more lately. They smoke pot and occasionally drop acid. Now some of them are thinking of trying mescaline and some of the other drugs. You don't know very much about drugs. You're not sure you believe what you have heard in the drug education programs at school. But you're scared right now. Sometimes you wonder if maybe you're hooked on the drugs, but you just don't know. You like this group of friends, and you feel less and less able to break out and leave them, but the group is getting more involved in drugs with each passing week.

Today, your cousin, who is a couple of years older than you, came by. You have felt closer to this cousin than most of the kids in your school, who are complete strangers. You feel you can trust him to talk with.

FRIEND TO DONNA

Today you drop by your aunt's house. Your cousin Donna is home. Donna has never had a lot of friends, but lately you know that she has been making some new friends in school. You feel good about that. You start talking. It turns out that she's bothered by something.

Role-Play Situation 4
KAY

You are 16 years old and pregnant. You are at a loss. You don't know what to do. You are afraid to tell your parents. They wouldn't understand, you feel. You'd like to tell Ken, but not really, because he might think that he'll have to marry you. You don't want him to marry you just because you're pregnant. You're not sure you want to marry him at all. You don't know who to turn to, and you feel so alone. The aloneness is the most frightening of all. You feel ashamed, and you don't have too many good feelings about yourself anyway. You often feel low esteem for yourself. Then there's the pregnancy: should you keep the baby, have an abortion, get married—or what?

Your friend Jill has been pretty close to you, and she seems to be someone you can trust. You decide to talk with her.

FRIEND TO KAY

You are Jill. Kay is a pretty good friend of yours. She's been kind of down in the dumps the last few days. Today she told you that she wants to talk with you after school. You see her now.

Role-Play Situation 5
JAKE

You are 18. You have just broken up with your girl friend, Ginny, and it's really hit you hard. You really need her and miss being with her, but when you're together you just can't seem to get along. When you were going with her, you would argue all the time and seem to hurt each other at every turn. It was mostly Ginny who decided that you should break up, but you were pretty much in agreement with it because you were so frustrated with what was happening between you. Now you don't know what to do, where to go. You just think about it all the time. You feel as if you'd like to give up.

Today you share this with a good friend of yours who always seems pretty open and understanding to you.

FRIEND TO JAKE

Jake is a good friend of yours. You've always been able to talk to each other about things that are important to you. This is one thing that has made the friendship very steady and good. Recently Jake and Ginny, his girl friend, broke up. He's been pretty down since then. Today you are talking together.

Role-Play Situation 6

JUDY

You are 19 years old. You have no job and just graduated from high school a few months ago. Not long after you finished school you met an older man who kind of turned you on. You have been living with him ever since then. But now you realize that you don't care about him any more. You would like to try and leave him but you feel stuck. Living with him has kind of felt like having a home —and you never felt you had a home when you lived with your parents. You know you can't go back to your parents. You're really scared. You want to leave, but you don't know if you dare. He'd really get angry if you left. You don't have anywhere to go or anything to go to. You're afraid of really being on your own— pretty scared to face life. You feel messed up—you can't seem to think straight any longer.

You go to talk to an old friend of yours that you know from high school.

FRIEND TO JUDY

Judy is someone you knew when you were in high school. You didn't know her well, but you used to have a pretty good relationship when you did see each other. She has come to you now, very upset, very frightened. She looks very mixed up. You want to try to help her.

Mini-Lecture: The Power of Acceptance

PURPOSE: to heighten an awareness of the need to give and receive acceptance

Here is a verbatim description of one way in which the idea of acceptance can be talked about:

When I feel accepted and understood in another's eyes, I no longer have to struggle to gain acceptance, or to assert my right to do or feel the way I do. When I feel accepted by others, I have a sense of belonging. It feels safe to be spontaneous—to honestly say what I feel, to create, and to explore the things I am interested in.

When I feel acceptance of others, I feel free—free from coercion to be other than I am, free to be and to explore my own being—to live or seek the life that I find good and meaningful.

Lack of acceptance, on the other hand, is something I may sense coming from my parents, my teachers, or from some segments of my peer group. I feel their lack of acceptance as a judgment that says I am not worthwhile as I am right now; that in some ways, I am inferior, bad, no good, deficient.

When I feel this way I may be afraid to act—to try new things—to do anything that might meet with their disapproval. I feel pinched inside. It is hard to dance, sing, shout with joy, when I feel disapproval from others.

The kind af acceptance I would like to have is one which will let me become—one in which you will let me happen, change, and not have to adhere to your expectations for what you think I ought to be.

Announcements

Set a meeting place and time for the next session.

Remind everyone to cut out pictures of people from magazines before the next meeting. These pictures of people should be ones to which they have a reaction of "I like this person, the way he/she looks, or what he is doing," or "I don't like this person, the way he/

she looks, or what he is doing." They will be using the pictures as a main focus for the next session. To be sure they remember their pictures you could call them a couple of days before the next meeting. Otherwise, many forget and you may spend at least half of the meeting waiting while they cut out pictures.

Goal Reporting, Goal Setting

PURPOSE: to establish a pattern of conscious goal selection and achievement

to reinforce successful goal fulfillment by sharing with other group members

Last session each of the group members identified an area he wanted to focus on to strengthen his goal-setting practice. Now, in the total group ask each person to tell what he selected as a goal, why he selected it, and how it went for him.

When everyone has reported on his past week's goal, ask each person to find a partner and work in pairs to select a goal for the coming week.

Closing

SESSION 8: MY RESPONSE TO OTHERS

Sharing Where I Am
Repeat this experience as described in Session 1.

People I Like and Don't Like
PURPOSE: to increase and dramatize awareness of our instant, un-
thought-through reactions to other people

to discover the objectionable and the desirable in others
and in ourselves through seeing it first in others

to increase the probability of greater understanding and
insight into our reactions to other people

This exercise can help the participants begin to identify to what
extent they like and dislike in other people the very qualities which
are a part of themselves. It may also provide a greater sensitivity
for some of the people to whom they have strong positive or
negative reactions.

The following series of tasks gets a little complicated, but it is
worth following the instructions as closely as possible. The group
should subdivide into groups of not over four. If they chose subgroups during the retreat, these would be good working groups for
this task. When you introduce this task to the group, go through
the instructions carefully, using pictures you have selected for yourself as an example.

Tape up a sheet of newsprint, and using a few examples among a
number of pictures you have taped on to it, run through the exercises described in the following instructions.

Arranging the Pictures

Pictures should be arranged on the newsprint as shown in this illustration. When each person in your subgroup has his materials arranged in this way, take turns going through the following sequence with your pictures. One person shares at a time while the others listen and help the person who is talking explore his responses.

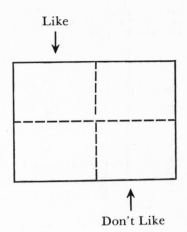

Like

Don't Like

Working with the "Don't Like" Section

You start by focusing your attention on the "Don't Like" section only. Here you do three things.

- Talk to each picture in this section, or tell the members of your group how you feel about each picture in the section. Talk about how you feel about them and how they affect you. *Example:* When I see her sad eyes I feel depressed and hopeless. I feel like going away to a corner somewhere and just sitting.

- Now have other members of the subgroup identify for the person who is talking about his pictures the characteristics of people who most turn him off—whom he most dislikes. Write these characteristics in the lower left hand space of the newsprint.

- The person who is talking about his pictures will now look at each picture in the "Don't Like" section and describe when he is most like each of these persons—when he displays the same characteristics. *Example:* I am like him when I am afraid and angry.

Working with the "Like" Section

Focus now on the "Like" section of your newsprint sheet. Go through the same series of interactions with the pictures as you did for the "Don't Like" section.

- Talk about how you feel about each person, and how the feeling affects you.
- Other members of the group identify the characteristics of the persons whom he likes and writes them in the upper right hand space on the newsprint.
- Now identify when you are most like the persons in each picture.

Identifying What I'm Like
When all the characteristics of the persons in the "Like" and the "Don't Like" sections are written down, the person talking about his pictures will circle the words on the sheet which he feels are also characteristics of him.

Talking About It
When each person has finished going through the series of explorations on the pictures he selected as "Like" and "Don't Like," bring the group together to talk about the experience. What did they learn about the people's characteristics that they especially like and don't like? What does it tell them about themselves?

Announcements
Set the meeting time and place for the next session. Be sure to save the newsprint sheets with the pictures on them. This will also be used in the next section.

Goal Reporting and Goal Setting
PURPOSE: to establish a pattern of conscious goal selection and achievement

to reinforce successful goal fulfillment by sharing with other group members

Goals were set at the last session with a partner. It may be a valuable experience to do goal setting with one other person for the rest of the sessions. Invite the group members to find a partner that they would like to do goal setting with for the rest of the sessions. With this partner, they will report on their outcome on the goal they selected at the last session and then set another goal for the coming week. Ask them to think again of the kind of things they would like to have accomplished by the time the series is over. This may help to direct their goal setting.

Closing

There are just two sessions left. Does this influence the kind of closing you want to choose?

SESSION 9: VALUES AND ACCEPTANCE FOR OTHERS AND FOR ME

Where I Am
Repeat this experience as described in Session 1.

What I Value in Life
PURPOSE: to gain further understanding of my perception of what other people are like

to discover more about how I am like or unlike others

This exercise builds on the *People I Like and Don't Like* sheets which were made the previous week. In addition, each person will need some small scraps of paper and tape in order to put additional words on their sheets.

The same subgroups that met together for the last session can be used, as this is a continuation of the previous task. Each person will begin by working by himself, and then sharing his outcomes with the other members of the subgroup.

Demonstrate the following procedures on your own set of pictures to make sure it is clear to the group.

- Begin with your newsprint sheet from last session with pictures of people you like and don't like. Next to or on each picture, tape a small piece of paper. On the paper write three things that you think may be most important in life to this person. For example, you may write the three words "prestige," "money," and "smart clothes" as three things you think may be most important to the kind of person one of your pictures represents. When you are finished, each person in your pictures will have three words or things that you guess are probably most important written on or beside him/his picture.

- Now go over all the words you wrote down and circle those which are also important to you. If there are other things which you consider as most important that your pictures have not shown, write those on the side of the sheet and circle them.

- When you have finished, look over what you have done and see what you can learn about yourself.

- Talk with the other members of your subgroup to discuss what each of you found by doing this.

Mini-Lecture: Different Ways of Valuing in Life

PURPOSE: to sharpen awareness of the difficulty in imposing our value systems on other people

to raise the issue of how to view and relate to others who are different from us

These are the basic ideas to communicate about valuing. One way to do this is in a dialogue demonstration between you and one of the pictures on your newsprint sheet. You can talk about the potential value conflict between one of the people in your "Don't Like" section and yourself.

You and I may value life on a different basis. I have a certain set of values which describe for me what I think is important in life. It is in part these values that influence me to live my life in the ways I do.

Sometimes I think, "This is what is really important in life." Because it is important to me, I want other people to also think and live the way I would like them to—in a way that fits what I think is important.

Let's take a look at you for a minute. No doubt you think you know what is really important in life. You are convinced that what you value is important, and that I should see and do things your way—because, I suppose, you also think you are right.

What are we going to do about the things you think I ought to do and the things I think are so important that you seem to consider unimportant or mistaken?

There are so many different ways of doing and being in life. Each person seems to feel that his way is the way he wants things to be. And so do you and I. And so does a world of people who value the being and doing part of life somewhat differently than we do.

Invite the group to talk about values, and what happens when two different persons or groups of persons value a way of life that conflicts with one another's.

Accepting You and Me

PURPOSE: to offer an opportunity for openness in sharing self-perceived good and bad characteristics in ourselves

to provide an experience of acceptance by others and self

During the past two sessions, focus has been on an exploration of some things group members can discover about themselves by examining their attitudes toward others. Perhaps the most important learning throughout these exercises is some new awareness of some of one's own not-so-obvious attributes.

Growing out of these experiences, this exercise is an opportunity for simple, honest sharing of knowing and accepting one another.

Demonstrate this procedure for the group by doing it with one of the group members.

Sit down with a partner. As you talk together, make a special effort to be simple and sincere in your communication. Look over your partner's sheet of pictures with all the words circled that are descriptive of what he thinks he is like. Comment briefly.

You say you are _____ [*angry, idealistic, loving selfish*]. *I see these—all the things you say you are—and I accept you. You're OK.*

It's very important to be honest with your partner. Don't say anything you don't really mean. If you're not ready to accept your partner, discuss it with him.

103

As each person shares with a partner, it is important to take *his* word for what he says he is like. The point for each person is: do you accept this person, seeing and knowing what he is like as he has described himself?

When the pair has exchanged evaluations, they should change partners until they have shared with all the people they want to communicate acceptance to.

There will not be time for all people to exchange declarations of acceptance. When the time runs out, have the group sit in a circle.

Self Acceptance

When the group is seated in the circle, start with the leader as a model for this next phase. Do a kind of *Where I Am* in relation to the experience you have just had. If each person honestly can, encourage them to affirm themselves as others have affirmed them:

I see myself as _____ *and I accept myself. I'm OK.*

Goal Reporting and Goal Setting

PURPOSE: to reinforce successful goal fulfillment by sharing with other group members

to direct attention toward a selection of a long-range goal

to firm up any areas of goal setting and goal fulfillment which have not felt satisfactory so far.

Point out to the group that this session is the last time they will be setting a short-range goal. It is an opportunity to check out the goal setting they have done so far and select a goal in an area they want to strengthen.

During the next session they will be encouraged to select a long-range goal. Tell them about this now so they can put some thought into their selection if they wish to. One possible choice for this session's goal might be to make an exploratory attempt at the kind of thing they may want to do for a long-range goal.

Have the group members meet with the same partners they had last session for goal setting, report their progress on their goal for that week, and set another one for the next session.

Announcements
Set place and time for the next meeting. Remind the group that it will be the last meeting of the PEER series.

Closing

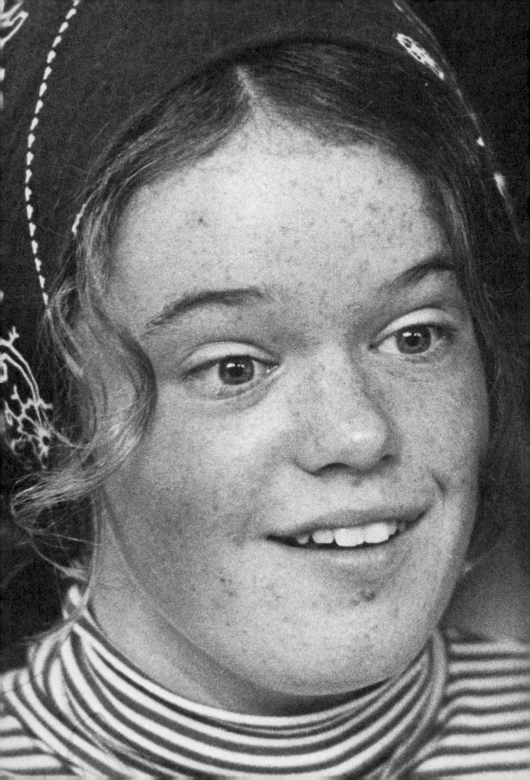

SESSION 10: WHERE I GO FROM HERE

Where I Am

Repeat this experience as described in Session 1.

Announcements

Make any announcements you need to provide for the group at this time.

Review of PEER

PURPOSE: to review the total series, its basic goals and assumptions. Explain that since this is the last meeting of the series, it may be valuable to look back at the group's experiences. Invite people to talk some about some of the highlights of their experiences. Then offer a kind of summary of the primary principles in relationships which have been a focus of this series. Here is an account of what a summary might be like:

> *The primary focus throughout the series has been on relationships. The key to your relationship is—how do I feel about myself? From the basis of your caring-acceptance of yourself, you reach out to care for other people.*
>
> *Our experiences have basically been structured around a gradual knowing and sharing of ourselves with each other. Many of us have found that as we learn to know ourselves and one another more fully, we can also learn to understand, care for, and accept ourselves and each other as persons.*
>
> *We have practiced some communication skills which can help us to share more fully and more accurately in a relationship. We have learned to share what we are experiencing, our inner reality—and what the other person is experiencing.*
>
> *At the core of this kind of communication, this kind of being people together, is a way of experiencing and relating to other*

people. What we hope for is that we can honestly and openly
address others from a basis of

> *my experience of me,*
> *my experience of you,*
> *my experience of us.*

We do this by being in touch with and being personal in relation
to me, you, and us. Then we can experience it as

> *I share me—offer myself as vulnerable, open to you,*
> *I invite you—to tell me, share with me,*
> *I address you from the possibility of a "we."*

When we do this we may change our basic way of being in
life from an objective, impersonal attitude to a touching, per-
sonal becoming.

We've had some good experiences together in these past weeks.
We've been exploring some other ways of being together in rela-
tionships. Tonight we'll spend some time looking ahead—to what
we would like to have happen in the future—in our own personal
lives. We'll look for some ways to make relationships work in
other times and other places with other people.

Being in Relationships

PURPOSE: to provide a review of the skills taught for use in relationships

to help group members to identify some ways they feel
they may be helpful to other people through a relationship

This series focused on reflective listening skills as well as the skill of
sharing our feelings through an "I" message. The group has practiced these through some role-play situations. Now it will be important for group members to be able to incorporate these skills
into their conversational patterns so that all the relationships they
have can be enriched when these skills are used.

Ask for two volunteers who are willing to have a conversation and
skill practice session which the others can observe. Then ask them

108

to talk about how they feel about having taken part in the training series and how they hope to use the training they have had. As they exchange their feelings and ideas, encourage them to use their skills of reflective listening and "I" messages as a part of their conversation. As a part of the natural flow of the conversation, they should attempt to reflect one another's feelings and talk about their own feelings in response to each other.

After this modeling situation, the group may wish to discuss the experience briefly and then divide into pairs to carry out the same interchange throughout the group.

When they are through, have them discuss what application of the communication skills can add to relationships they have at present. What kinds of impact might they make on new relationships?

Ideas About Relationships

PURPOSE: to stimulate some further thinking about some factors involved in relationships

By now, group members have had many experiences in deepening relationships among themselves. As they think about making serious efforts to extend friendship to individuals outside the group, it may be helpful to talk further about the concrete ways in which friendship is extended, the possibility of risk involved, and how you balance the risk against the gain.

What are the specific things you do in initiating and fostering a relationship with another person? Think of a person you'd like to start a friendship with. Think how it might go.

It begins as you single out another person for attention.
You begin to talk.
You are sensitive to what he is saying—both verbally and nonverbally.
You communicate mutual understanding and acceptance (if it's there).
You show this through gestures, eyes, your words, etc.

You initiate a future contact.

You do or give little things that show you are valued by each other.

You do things together which you both enjoy.

How does it feel to be troubled? What kind of help can you offer such a person, and how does it help? Suppose I am troubled and hurting. Think how I must be feeling, and how you might reach out to me.

I am alone. When you sit beside me during my aloneness, my pain, that helps.

I may invite you to be near me, or you may sense my aloneness and offer to be near me.

When you are with me in my trouble, you may not know how to help me, but you can accept the invitation to be together with me while I make the journey.

You cannot take on my trouble, my pain. You may not even want to. But if you are near me as I go through it—trying to understand—it helps.

Both of these actions—extending friendship to another person, and extending comfort to someone who is hurting—involve some possibility of risk. There is the chance, all along, that the person may turn you off, laugh at you, turn his back. And that hurts. But it helps to know that the reasons for his doing it may come out of his feeling of loneliness, his feeling of hurt, rather than as a response to what you are offering. It's too bad, but it sometimes happens, so it is good to know ahead of time that it may, and to take the risk, anyway.

Where Do I Grow From Here?

PURPOSE: to help group members begin to work on building a support base for themselves which will continue for them when the group is no longer available for them.

This is a time to think through those experiences that have been valuable in this group, that have resulted in learning for us. It is a time to think about how we can make what we have learned useful in other times and places, with other people.

This is an individual task in which each person may seek to create his own way to do it. The next segment of time is unstructured so that each person can develop his own thing in his own way.

Here is a suggested way to handle the task:

- Each person will be seeking to identify how he wishes to be in relationships—if and how he wishes to grow—and how he will take what he has experienced here and make it work for him in other relationships outside of this group.
- Each person should work in any way that is useful for him. People may choose to work by themselves, or in twos, or in small groups.
- Some specific questions they might investigate could include: What have I gained that I'd like to keep? When I feel myself slipping, where, or to whom, can I go? How can I continue to use this group or some of its members as a support system for me? Where can I build a support system for myself outside of this group?

After the work session is completed, gather the group together to discuss and share the individual planning that has occurred. During discussion, take opportunities to stress the following points:

- need for solidifying and generalizing learning to make it a part of your own life
- highlight workable ideas offered which broaden the support base for group members outside the group itself
- advisability of selecting people for relationships who show a high chance of success at first
- setting limited, realistically selected goals
- the need for taking a certain amount of risk in establishing relationships

Long Range Goal Setting

to direct attention toward a long-range goal for each
member

During the previous session, the group was told that they would
be talking about long-range goals at this session. Share these in the
total group at this session. The goals may be 1 to 5 years into the
future, or, if they prefer, a few months. Make this sharing as
leisurely and supportive as feels good. This exercise is a way of
saying goodbye and points its members toward the future.

Closing

If it feels appropriate for your group, you may share once more
Where I Am with the group.